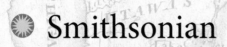

Smithsonian

Exploring
the
Connecticut
Colony

by Steven Otfinoski

CAPSTONE PRESS
a capstone imprint

11/17
23.99

Smithsonian Books are published by Capstone Press,
1710 Roe Crest Drive, North Mankato, Minnesota 56003
www.capstonepub.com

Library of Congress Cataloging-in-Publication Data
Names: Otfinoski, Steven, author.
Title: Exploring the Connecticut Colony / by Steven Otfinoski.
Description: North Mankato, Minnesota: Capstone Press, [2017] | Series:
   Smithsonian. Exploring the 13 colonies | Includes bibliographical
   references and index. | Audience: Ages 8-11.
Identifiers: LCCN 2016008182| ISBN 9781515722403 (library binding) | ISBN
   9781515722533 (pbk.) | ISBN 9781515722663 (ebook (.pdf))
Subjects: LCSH: Connecticut—History—Colonial period, ca.
   1600–1775—Juvenile literature. | Connecticut—History—Revolution,
   1775–1783—Juvenile literature.
Classification: LCC F97 .O84 2017 | DDC 974.6/02—dc23
LC record available at http://lccn.loc.gov/2016008182

Editorial Credits
Gina Kammer, editor; Richard Parker, designer; Eric Gohl, media researcher;
Kathy McColley, production specialist

Our very special thanks to Stephen Binns at the Smithsonian Center for Learning and Digital Access for
his curatorial review. Capstone would also like to thank Kealy Gordon, Smithsonian Institution Product
Development Manager, and the following at Smithsonian Enterprises: Christopher A. Liedel, President;
Carol LeBlanc, Senior Vice President; Brigid Ferraro, Vice President; Ellen Nanney, Licensing Manager.

Photo Credits
Alamy: The National Trust Photolibrary, 20; Capstone: 8; The Connecticut Women's Hall of Fame:
32; CriaImages.com: Jay Robert Nash Collection, 34, 35 (top); David R. Wagner: 38; Getty Images:
Hulton Archive, 5, Print Collector, 19, Stringer/Hulton Archive, 13, Stringer/MPI, 12; Granger, NYC:
11; Library of Congress: 10, 17, 37; New York Public Library: 39; Newscom: World History Archive,
41; North Wind Picture Archives: cover, 4, 6–7, 14, 15, 16, 18, 21, 22, 24, 25, 26, 27, 28, 29, 30, 31, 33, 35
(bottom), 36; Yale University Art Gallery: 23

Design Elements: Shutterstock

Printed and bound in the USA.
009669F16

Table of Contents

The 13 Colonies 4

Native Peoples of Connecticut 10

A Colony Is Founded 14

The Colony Grows 20

The Land of Steady Habits 26

The Road to Revolution and Statehood 34

Timeline 42

Glossary 44

Critical Thinking Using
    the Common Core 45

Read More 45

Internet Sites 45

Source Notes 46

Select Bibliography 47

Index 48

Introduction:
The 13 Colonies

Connecticut is one of 13 Colonies that England established on the Atlantic coast of what is now the United States. A **colony** is a land settled by people from another country. The government and economy of the colony is controlled by the home country of the settlers.

The English were latecomers in the settling of the Americas. The Spanish, Portuguese, and French came before them. The Spanish conquered most of what is now called Latin America. The French would claim much of what is now Canada and the central United States. For the most part, the Spanish and French came looking for wealth, whether in the form of gold and silver or fish and furs.

French ships set sail for Canada in the 1500s.

Early settlers build their fort in Jamestown, Virginia.

Why They Came

The English settlers came for many different reasons. Some left home to find new opportunities to practice the skills of a trade. Some wanted land they could farm and call their own, instead of farming for large landholders in England. Some hoped to be large landholders themselves. Others came so that they could worship freely, which they couldn't do at home. The first permanent English colony was established at Jamestown, Virginia, in 1607. The second, the Plymouth Colony (which later became part of Massachusetts), was set up by the Pilgrims in 1620.

colony—a place that is settled by people from another country and is controlled by that country.

Growth and Change

The early colonists faced many hardships. They had to deal with hotter summers and colder winters than they knew in England. They had to grow their own food. When crops failed, they starved. Native Americans were a great help to the earliest colonists. However, relations became less friendly as the Native Americans lost more and more of their homeland to the colonists.

Despite the challenges, each colony grew and developed. Newer settlers were not all from England. They also came from other places in Europe, such as the Netherlands, Germany, Scotland, Ireland, and Sweden. Villages grew into towns, and large towns became small cities.

At first the colonies had little contact with one another. But as roads got better, travel became easier. The colonies traded with one another. They also supported each other in defending the English settlements as a whole.

CONNECTICUT

The first colonists in America faced hard winters in unfamiliar lands. They had to start their lives over, building homes and setting up farms in a world strange and new to them.

Each region of Colonial America developed in its own way. The Northern Colonies were home to skilled craftsmen, fishermen, and small farmers who worked the rocky soil. The soil of the Middle Colonies was good for growing wheat and corn. The soil and climate of the Southern Colonies were better for growing tobacco, rice, cotton, or **indigo**. Those profitable crops were grown on large farms, called **plantations**. Slaves brought from Africa performed most of the labor on plantations. There were fewer manufacturers or other businesses in the South.

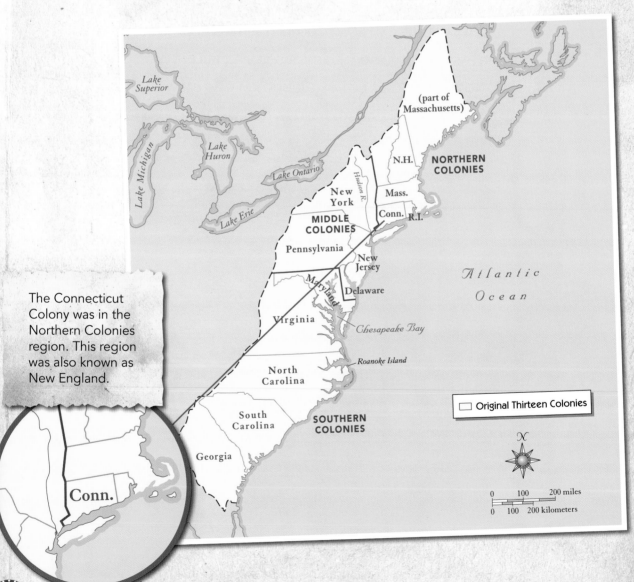

The Connecticut Colony was in the Northern Colonies region. This region was also known as New England.

The Original 13 Colonies

The first permanent European settlement in each colony:

Colony	Year	Colony	Year
Virginia	1607	Delaware	1638
Massachusetts	1620	Pennsylvania	1643
New Hampshire	1623	North Carolina	1653
New York	1624	New Jersey	1660
Connecticut	1633	South Carolina	1670
Maryland	1634	Georgia	1733
Rhode Island	1636		

Throughout the 1600s and into the 1700s, the colonies continued to grow and flourish, and new colonies were founded. Georgia, the last of the 13 Colonies, was founded in 1733. By then each region had its own culture and way of life different from England and different from each other. Connecticut developed into one of the most independent of the colonies. Early on it established its own written rules of government called a constitution. However, all of the colonies relied on England for most of their goods and trade.

indigo—a plant that produces a deep-blue dye
plantation—a large farm where crops are raised by people who live there

Chapter 1:
Native Peoples
of Connecticut

Connecticut was not an empty wilderness when the first European colonists arrived. In the early 1600s, there may have been about 30,000 Native Americans living there. **Ancestors** of these Native Americans first came to the region about 10,000 years ago.

An Algonquian People

Connecticut's native people shared a common language group, Algonquian, even though they lived in separate tribes. The Tunxis, Podunks, and Poquonnocs lived in central Connecticut. The Quinnipiacs inhabited the south-central region near present-day New Haven. The Paugussetts and Siwanogs lived in the southwest, and the Pequots and the Mohegans lived in the southeast. The Nipmunks were from the northeast. In the first few years, there was little violence between Connecticut colonists and native people.

This engraving from the early 1600s shows farms and homes in an Algonquian village.

Daily Life

Connecticut's Native Americans lived by farming, fishing, and hunting. Many lived in semi-permanent villages. They followed the animals they hunted from season to season. These animals included deer, moose, ducks, turkeys, and rabbits. They also hunted wolves and foxes for their fur, which the women made into clothing.

Both men and women planted fields of corn, squash, and beans. At harvesttime the women picked the crops. Children gathered nuts and wild berries to add to their meals. The men fished for salmon, sturgeon, and other fish in the rivers and Long Island Sound. They traveled on water in canoes they made from tree trunks. The women and children gathered clams, oysters, and other shellfish in the shallow waters of Long Island Sound.

This early engraving depicts Algonquian men fishing from canoes.

Did You Know?

The name "Connecticut" comes from a Mohegan word that means "beside the long river."

ancestor—a member of a person's family who lived a long time ago

At Home and At Play

Connecticut's native people lived in **wigwams**, or dome-shaped houses. To build a house, they placed saplings in a circle and tied the tops together. Then they usually covered the structure with tree bark. A fire could be lit inside the wigwam for warmth and cooking. A hole at the top allowed the smoke to escape.

The Native Americans made baskets, spears, canoes, and other useful articles. They also made dolls out of cornhusks. When they weren't working, they enjoyed telling stories. The children played games with balls or shot at targets with their bows and arrows.

An artist imagined an Algonquian medicine man at work in his wigwam.

Did You Know?

Native American chiefs in eastern North America were called sachems. The word comes from one of the Algonquian languages.

Tribal Tensions

When the first colonists arrived in Connecticut, most Native Americans welcomed them in peace. They were willing to help the newcomers, hoping they would protect them from their enemy, the Pequots. Unfortunately the Europeans brought diseases such as measles and **smallpox** with them. The Native Americans had no defenses against these diseases. About half of Connecticut's native population—as many as 15,000—died within years of the colonists' arrival.

The Pequots resented the colonists, who were beginning to take their land from them. Tensions between the colonists and the Pequots would eventually lead to war.

Samson Occom (1723–1792)

Colonists **converted** many Native Americans to Christianity. The best known of these converts in Connecticut was Samson Occom of the Mohegan tribe. He was born near New London in 1723 and converted while in his teens. Occom was educated by the Reverend Eleazor Wheelock and later became a minister in the Presbyterian Church. He traveled to England to help raise money for Wheelock's school for Native Americans. This school would later become Dartmouth College in New Hampshire. Occom moved to New York where he taught the Oneidas. He started an independent Christian Oneida community called Brothertown, where he lived until his death in 1792.

wigwam—a hut made of poles covered with bark, leaves, or animal skins

smallpox—a disease that spreads easily from person to person, causing chills, fever, and pimples that scar

convert—to change from one religion or faith to another

Chapter 2:
A Colony Is Founded

Dutch trader Adriaen Block and his crew were the first Europeans to explore Connecticut. They had been exploring the Hudson River region in present-day New York on their ship *Onrust* (meaning "Restless" in Dutch) in 1614. Then they crossed Long Island Sound and sailed up the Connecticut River. Block called it the *Versch Rivier*, meaning "Fresh River." He traveled up the river about 60 miles north of present-day Hartford. Passing Native American villages, he saw the potential for trading furs with the people.

Block claimed the land for the Netherlands, his home country. But it took about 10 years for other Dutch adventurers to set up a small trading post. The post was located at the mouth of the Connecticut River at present-day Old Saybrook. Almost 10 years later, the Dutch established a small fort at present-day Hartford that they called the "House of Good Hope." But there was little hope for the Dutch in Connecticut. When English colonists from Massachusetts arrived, the Dutch abandoned their fort.

A Dutch ship sails near the House of Good Hope.

Massachusetts colonists traveled south to settle in Wethersfield and Windsor.

The Three River Towns

Englishmen from Plymouth Colony in Massachusetts learned of the good fur trade in the Connecticut River Valley. In 1633 they sailed up the Connecticut River to settle near the land the Dutch had claimed. They brought the parts of a pulled-down house with them and quickly rebuilt the house on a site north of Hartford. They wanted to make their own claim known to the Dutch. The settlers then surrounded the house with a small fort and called the place Windsor. It was the first permanent English settlement in Connecticut.

Some **Puritans** found the religious laws in Massachusetts too strict. They decided to leave to form their own rules. One group headed south to found their own settlement, which they called Wethersfield, in present-day Connecticut. Then in 1636 Puritan pastor Thomas Hooker led another group to found Hartford. Windsor, Wethersfield, and Hartford became known as the "Three River Towns" because they all lay along the Connecticut River.

Puritan—a follower of a strict religion common during the 1500s and 1600s; Puritans wanted simple church services and enforced a strict moral code

CONNECTICUT

The Pequot War

The Pequots felt threatened by the colonists who were taking over their land. In April 1637 around 200 Pequots attacked colonists working in a field in Wethersfield, killing nine people.

The colonists decided to strike back. John Mason and John Underhill led an army of Connecticut and Massachusetts volunteers. Their **allies**, Mohegan and Narragansett warriors, joined them. On May 26, 1637, they reached a Pequot stronghold near present-day Mystic, Connecticut. During the fierce fighting, Mason gave the order to burn the fort. As many as 700 Pequots, mostly women, children, and old men, burned to death or were shot trying to escape the burning fort. A few of the Pequots escaped. But during the Pequot War, many others were captured, sold into slavery, and sent to the West Indies. Some of the survivors' descendants still live in Connecticut today.

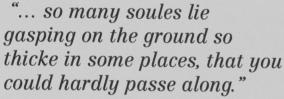

"... so many soules lie gasping on the ground so thicke in some places, that you could hardly passe along."
—Captain John Underhill describing the scene after the massacre, 1638

In 1637 John Mason's army destroyed a Pequot fort, including the women and children inside.

Critical Thinking with Primary Sources

This illustration from 1638 shows the attack on the Pequot fort the previous year. Why was there no escape for the Pequots inside the fort once it was set on fire? Notice the Native Americans holding bows and arrows standing behind the soldiers. Who do you think they are?

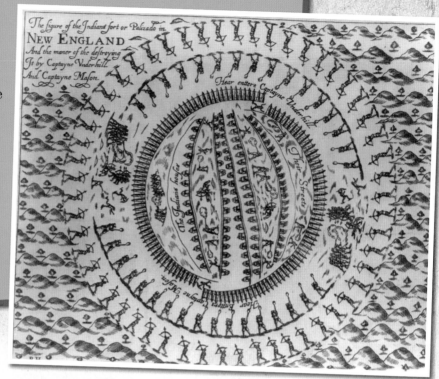

New Haven Colony

In 1638 the River Towns planned to join together to form the Connecticut Colony. The same year another group of Puritans arrived in Connecticut led by Reverend John Davenport. Unlike the founders of the Three River Towns, these people left Massachusetts because they thought it was too **liberal**. They founded the settlement of New Haven with a government based on their Congregational religion. The Congregationalists were Puritan **Protestants** who believed each church should run itself.

Did You Know?

The American-built ship *Desire* brought Pequots to the West Indies as slaves. That same ship returned with Connecticut's first African slaves.

ally—a person or country that helps and supports another

liberal—broad-minded and tolerant, especially of other people's ideas

Protestant—a Christian who does not belong to the Roman Catholic or the Orthodox Church

The Fundamental Orders

In 1639 Reverend Thomas Hooker and other Puritan leaders wrote and adopted a document called the Fundamental Orders. It laid out the laws that would govern the Connecticut Colony. Among the rights it gave to citizens was the right to vote, whether they belonged to the Congregational Church or not. However, the right to vote did not extend to women, Native Americans, or African-Americans. Some people have called the Fundamental Orders the world's first written constitution. The document even earned Connecticut one of its nicknames, the Constitution State.

> *"… the foundation of authority is laid, firstly, in the free consent of the people."*
> —Thomas Hooker in a sermon delivered on May 31, 1638

Thomas Hooker and his followers settle on the Connecticut River.

The war fought in England brought many changes to the American Colonies.

Two Colonies

Other colonies joined together with the Connecticut Colony, including the short-lived Saybrook Colony in 1644. However, the New Haven Colony resisted. It wanted to keep its independence from the more liberal colony to its north. As the Connecticut Colony grew, so did the New Haven Colony. The shoreline towns of Guilford and Branford to the east joined the New Haven Colony. Milford, Stamford, and Greenwich to the west also joined.

Both colonies enjoyed a large degree of independence while England was busy fighting in the English Civil War (1642–1651). The war began as a struggle for power between the king and Parliament—England's lawmaking body. The Puritans in England, who sided with Parliament, wanted more religious freedom. Parliament took control of England, but this rule without a king lasted only a decade. The **monarchy** was restored in 1660 when King Charles II came to the throne. This would bring new changes to life in the American Colonies.

monarchy—a system of government in which the ruler is a king or queen

Chapter 3:
The Colony Grows

When King Charles II came to power in 1660, he tried to gain strict authority over his colonies. The Connecticut Colony was quick to respond. It sent Governor John Winthrop, Jr. as its representative to England in 1661. The next year the king granted Winthrop a **charter**, which gave the colony a surprising degree of self-government. The Connecticut Colony could elect its own governor and other leaders. The charter also gave Connecticut a strip of land that ran from coast to coast—from Narragansett Bay (now part of Rhode Island) all the way to the Pacific Ocean! No one at the time knew how much land lay in between.

Did You Know?

In 1701 Connecticut's General Assembly made New Haven the co-capital with Hartford. The General Assembly met in Hartford in May and in New Haven in October.

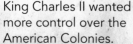

King Charles II wanted more control over the American Colonies.

End of a Colony

The charter also made the New Haven Colony part of the Connecticut Colony. At first the Puritans of New Haven resisted becoming part of the Connecticut Colony, but they finally surrendered in 1665. After nearly 25 years, the New Haven Colony was no more. A small group of people left New Haven rather than be part of the Connecticut Colony. They moved southwest and founded Newark, New Jersey.

Connecticut colonists discuss the charter given by King Charles II.

charter—an official document granting permission to set up a new colony, organization, or company

The Witch Trials

The Connecticut Colony was more liberal than the Massachusetts Bay Colony and the former New Haven Colony. However, superstition played a part in life throughout the colonies. Witches were real for people in the 1600s. Many innocent people were accused of performing evil deeds for Satan. Although the Salem witch trials in Massachusetts are more widely known, the first recorded witch trial in Colonial America took place in Connecticut. In 1647 Alice Young of Windsor was found guilty of witchcraft and was hanged. In 1662 nine people were tried as witches and four were found guilty and hanged. The last witch trial in the Northern Colonies took place in Connecticut in 1697. Laws against witchcraft, however, remained in effect until 1750.

Colonists arrest a woman accused of being a witch.

Critical Thinking with Primary Sources

This engraving shows John Winthrop, Jr. as a young man. It was made by Amos Doolittle after a painting of Winthrop. What does this portrait show about Winthrop's character? Why would people in Colonial times have painted or engraved portraits made of themselves?

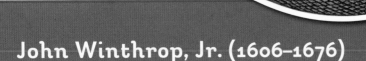

John Winthrop, Jr. (1606–1676)

One person who opposed the witch trials and helped to end them was Governor John Winthrop, Jr. Winthrop was a gifted scientist as well as an able politician. He didn't think every strange thing that happened was the work of the devil. He made a law that required more than just one witness to accuse someone of witchcraft. Winthrop helped establish and then governed the short-lived colony of Saybrook. He also founded the town of Pequot, which was later renamed New London. John Winthrop served as governor of Connecticut from 1659 until his death in 1676. His son later became governor as well.

Saving the Charter

In 1685 a new English king, James II, came to the throne. The king united all of the Northern Colonies—the region known as New England—into one big colony under his control. Sir Edmund Andros was to serve as the colony's royal governor. However, Connecticut did not want to join the so-called Dominion of New England. On October 31, 1687, Andros arrived in Hartford and demanded that the colonists turn over Connecticut's charter from 1662. Legend says that during the meeting between Andros and the colony's leaders, the candles went out. In the darkness, one colonist left the room with the charter and hid it in a nearby oak tree. Andros did not get the charter, and Connecticut never became part of the Dominion of New England. The tree, later known as the Charter Oak, was uprooted in a storm in 1856. But it is still a proud symbol of Connecticut today.

One of the Connecticut colonists hides the charter in an oak tree that would become known as the Charter Oak.

Slavery

African slaves were first brought to Hartford and New Haven around 1640. By 1730 Connecticut had a slave population of about 700. The enslaved people built homes, labored on farms, and worked in mills. Many wealthy people in Connecticut owned a slave or two, as did many middle-class people. But this was a small number compared to the Southern Colonies.

When the colonists later decided they wanted to be independent from England, they did not extend that freedom to African-American slaves. Even free black people and Native Americans were treated unfairly. For example, in 1690 a law was passed that said black people and Native Americans were not allowed on the streets after 9:00 p.m.

A hundred years later, in 1790, a Connecticut antislavery society was founded. A census that year showed there were about 2,700 slaves in Connecticut. But over the next 40 years, the number of enslaved people dwindled to 25. Slavery was finally **abolished** in the state in 1848.

Most people of wealth owned slaves in Colonial Connecticut.

Did You Know?

The frame that surrounds the Fundamental Orders in Hartford is made of wood taken from the Charter Oak.

abolish—

Chapter 4:
The Land of Steady Habits

Connecticut earned the nickname "the Land of Steady Habits" partly because the colony usually elected the same governor year after year, often until the governor died. But steady habits also referred to the hard work that helped make Connecticut and its people successful.

Manufacturing

By the early 1700s, Connecticut was a leader in manufacturing. Skilled craftsmen made tin and silver items, such as pans and mugs, in their shops. Shipbuilders made vessels to sail on the ocean and along rivers. Workers labored in **gristmills** and sawmills, grinding grain into flour and cutting trees into lumber used for building. Miners dug copper out of the earth.

A man works in a gristmill.

The middle class included shopkeepers.

Three Classes

Three classes of people emerged in Connecticut society. The upper class was made up of business owners and people who **inherited** their wealth. They held all the important posts in government. The middle class included everyone from artisans and shopkeepers to doctors and lawyers. Like the upper class, people of the middle class could vote in elections, but they rarely held political office. The lower class included semiskilled craftspeople, servants, and manual laborers. Many of these people were uneducated and could not read or write. Like women, African-Americans, and Native Americans, they were not allowed to vote.

gristmill—a building for grinding grain

inherit—to be given someone's property after he or she dies

Apprentices and Indentured Servants

Apprentices were mostly young men who agreed to work for a craftsman or tradesman in order to learn the business. They were not paid, but they were provided with food and housing. Between the ages of 14 and 21, most apprentices worked for someone else. At the end of that time, the employer helped the apprentice set up his own business.

Indentured servants were poor people who worked in exchange for passage to the colonies from Europe. When such servants arrived in the colonies, they lived with and worked for a master. This period of work usually lasted four to seven years. Then they were free to live and work on their own.

An indentured servant works alongside his master, a blacksmith.

Yankee Peddlers

Young men who didn't become apprentices often became peddlers. Peddlers sold Connecticut-made items and other goods from door to door. In their wagons they carried everything from cigars to cloth for making dresses. Like salesmen today these peddlers were persuasive talkers who knew how to make a sale. They became welcome figures in small villages and on farms where people had little opportunity to visit a store.

Some of these "Yankee peddlers" were less than honest. They sold clocks that soon stopped running and "silver spoons" that were really made of tin. They also sold nutmeg, a nutlike seed from Indonesia that, when grated, was a popular spice. It is said that some peddlers sold fake nutmeg made of wood. Nutmeg soon became associated with the peddlers and the colony they came from. Today Connecticut is still known as "the Nutmeg State."

apprentice—a person who works for another to learn a trade or craft

indentured servant—a person who works for someone else for a certain period of time in return for payment of travel and living costs

Work and Study

Daily life for most people in Colonial Connecticut consisted of hard work. While some colonists were employed at mills and small factories, most worked at home. Farmers worked in the fields, growing corn, squash, beans, and pumpkins. Craftsmen made goods in shops attached to their homes. Women cared for the home and the children. As the population grew in the 1700s, more and more people lived in towns rather than on farms.

Children were expected to help with chores in and around the home.

Most children not only went to school but also had daily chores. In 1650 a law was passed stating that every town of 50 families or more had to have a school. Education was important to the Connecticut colonists. The first college in Connecticut, the Collegiate School, opened in 1701 in Saybrook. It moved to New Haven in 1716 and was renamed Yale College in 1718. Today Yale is the third-oldest university in the United States.

Recreation and Religion

In Colonial times Sunday was a day of rest and worship. Congregationalists were required to attend services in the meetinghouse twice a week. On other days the meetinghouse served as a place for nonreligious meetings and elections. Men enjoyed gathering at inns to read the latest news and discuss political issues with their friends.

Colonists leave their meetinghouse after a church service.

Did You Know?

Created in 1764 the *Connecticut Courant* was a popular newspaper in the colonies. Now called the *Hartford Courant*, it is the oldest continuously running newspaper in the United States.

Women's Roles

Married women in Connecticut and other colonies were under the same laws as those in England. Any property, money, or inheritance a woman brought to the marriage automatically became her husband's. Single women, however, were allowed to own property. Women did gain some respect for the responsibilities they held at home and on the farm. Some women even ran businesses.

Hannah Bunce Watson (1749–1807)

When Ebenezer Watson, publisher of the *Connecticut Courant*, died in 1777, his wife, Hannah, took over the running of the newspaper. She managed to do this while raising five young children. In the paper Watson gave support to the **Patriots** during the American Revolution. She also showed a strong interest in scientific news. After she remarried she continued to publish the paper with her new husband and his business partner until her death in 1807.

New Tensions with England

By the mid-1700s many colonists thought of themselves not as English, and not only as subjects of the British Empire, but as Americans. Still, when the French and their Indian allies threatened the colonies, the colonists fought side by side with British soldiers. Great Britain won the French and Indian War (1754–1763) and gained much of France's land in North America. But the war was expensive, and Britain expected the colonies to help pay the war debt. Paper, tea, and other items were taxed. The colonists felt that these taxes, especially the Stamp Act of 1765, were unfair since the colonies had no say in the British government.

British soldiers fight in the French and Indian War. The war was expensive for England.

A secret group known as the Sons of Liberty formed to oppose the Stamp Act. In Boston they burned an effigy, or dummy, meant to represent one of the tax collectors. Other ways they protested included urging colonists and their local governments to avoid buying anything that the British could tax. These protests eventually led to the Revolutionary War.

Patriot—a person who sided with the colonies during the Revolutionary War

Chapter 5:
The Road to Revolution and Statehood

In April 1775 the Revolutionary War began with the Battles of Lexington and Concord in Massachusetts. When the first shots were fired, Connecticut was divided in its loyalties. Many colonists who lived east of the Connecticut River sided with the Patriots in Massachusetts. Many colonists who lived west of the Connecticut River shared the **Loyalist** values of many in neighboring New York—they remained loyal to England. This divided loyalty in Connecticut continued throughout the war.

About 41,000 Connecticut men served in the Continental army (the army of the Patriots) or the Connecticut **militia**. Most of the fighting in Connecticut was along the Atlantic coast. British troops stationed in New York crossed Long Island Sound in boats. They raided several towns, including New London, Norwalk, Fairfield, and, further inland, Danbury. They burned buildings and supplies and harassed the citizens. Their ships threatened the shores.

The Battles of Lexington and Concord were the first of the Revolutionary War.

The First Submarine

To strike back at the British ships that raided Connecticut's shore, inventor David Bushnell of Westbrook formed a plan. In 1776 he invented a submarine, the first to be used in wartime. Named the *Turtle*, it was made of two wooden shells bound together by iron hoops. It had just enough room inside for a pilot, who sat on a wooden plank. The pilot twisted a crank that turned a propeller, which moved the submarine either forward or backward. With explosives attached to the outside, the *Turtle* was supposed to sneak up on a British ship in New York Harbor. Then the pilot would attach the explosives to the underside of the ship and flee before the explosion. Unfortunately Bushnell and another pilot failed in several attempts to blow up a ship, and the *Turtle* has gone down in history as a brilliant but unsuccessful experiment.

This diagram of the *Turtle* shows what the early submarine might have looked like.

Nathan Hale (1755–1776)

When the war began, Nathan Hale of Coventry, Connecticut, was teaching school. He joined the Continental army and took part in battles in Boston. Soon after Hale volunteered to go behind enemy lines to gather information about British troops. The British captured him in New York several days later. On September 22, 1776, Hale was hanged without trial as a spy. He went to his death heroically and is remembered as a great Patriot.

Loyalist—a colonist who was loyal to Great Britain during the Revolutionary War

militia—a group of volunteer citizens who are organized to fight but are not professional soldiers

A Connecticut Traitor

Connecticut had its Revolutionary War heroes and its **traitors**. Since the beginning of the war, Benedict Arnold of Norwich, Connecticut, was a heroic and trusted American officer. He was wounded three times in the same leg, at the Battle of Quebec in Canada, the Battle of Ridgefield in Connecticut, and then during the important Patriot victory at Saratoga in New York. After Saratoga he was rewarded with command of the city of Philadelphia. But Arnold was bitter that other officers had been promoted over him. He was also losing faith in the American cause.

Influenced by his Loyalist wife, Arnold befriended **Tories** in Philadelphia and was scolded for this by the Pennsylvania government. Arnold was then ready to betray the American side. He got his opportunity when he was put in charge of the military base of West Point in New York. In 1780 Arnold offered to surrender West Point to the British. The plot failed, and Arnold fled to the British side. To this day calling someone a "Benedict Arnold" is another way of saying that the person is a traitor.

On September 6, 1781, Arnold led 1,700 British troops on a raid of New London, less than 15 miles from his hometown. Arnold took about half the troops into New London and easily captured Fort Trumbull there. Then he burned the town. The other British troops, led by Lieutenant Colonel Eyre and Major Montgomery, marched to nearby Fort Griswold in present-day Groton.

Benedict Arnold made a secret deal with the British and turned against the Americans.

Critical Thinking with Primary Sources

This 1781 sketch shows the attacks made on New London and Fort Griswold by Benedict Arnold. Can you find Fort Griswold? Where did the British troops march?

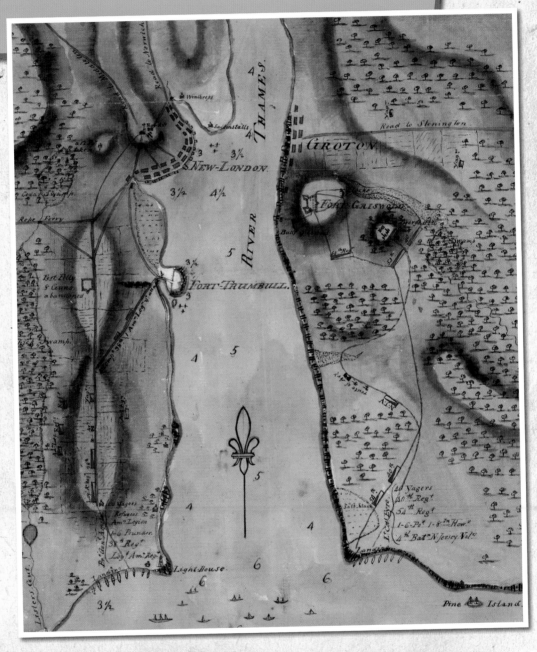

traitor—someone who aids the enemy of his or her country
Tory—a colonist who remained loyal to the British government

37

Massacre at Fort Griswold

Colonel William Ledyard defended Fort Griswold with 165 Patriots. The British demanded that Ledyard surrender the fort, but he refused.

The British outnumbered the defenders five to one, but the Americans fought fiercely. In the fighting Major Montgomery and other British officers were killed. Angered by the deaths of their commanders, the British showed no mercy after they took the fort. Ledyard offered his sword in defeat to the ranking British officer. But stories say that the officer stabbed Ledyard with his own sword, killing him. Altogether the British killed 85 men and wounded another 35.

After Benedict Arnold's betrayal, the Americans were defeated at Fort Griswold.

The next morning the departing British took some of the survivors back to New York as prisoners of war. It was the only major Revolutionary War battle fought on Connecticut soil and the last major battle fought in the Northern Colonies. About six weeks later, the British surrendered to the Americans at the Battle of Yorktown in Virginia.

> *"We will not give up the fort, let the consequences be what they may."*
>
> —Colonel Ledyard's reply to the British to surrender Fort Griswold, 1781

The Provision State

Because Connecticut was largely untouched by the war, its farmers were able to continue growing crops. These crops were sent to feed George Washington's Continental army. Connecticut's role in supplying the troops with food and other supplies was so great that Connecticut was called the "Provision State."

Governor Jonathan Trumbull, a good friend and trusted adviser to Washington, managed the sending of the supplies. He was the only Colonial governor to side with the Patriots and remain in office throughout the Revolutionary War. Washington thought so highly of Trumbull that when a problem arose in meetings with his staff, he would say, "We must ask Brother Jonathan."

Connecticut's Jonathan Trumbull (pictured) was well respected by George Washington.

The Connecticut Compromise

After Yorktown minor skirmishes continued for a time until final victory for the Americans came in 1783. The 13 Colonies were now independent states, but they were only weakly united under a document known as the Articles of Confederation.

In the summer of 1787, delegates from all of the states except Rhode Island met in Philadelphia and created a constitution for the new nation. One issue that they could not agree on was the structure of the lawmaking branch of the new government, Congress. Small states wanted the same number of representatives in Congress as the larger states. But the larger states didn't think that was fair. They wanted the number of representatives to be based on each state's population. This would give the large states more power in the government.

Roger Sherman, a delegate from Connecticut, came up with a compromise. There would be two branches of Congress. In the House of Representatives, the number of each state's representatives would be be based on that state's population. In the other branch, the Senate, all states would have equal representation—each state would have two senators. The delegates accepted this "Connecticut Compromise," and the U.S. Constitution was completed. Connecticut **ratified** the U.S. Constitution on January 9, 1788. It was the fifth state to do so. After a long and eventful history as a colony, the Nutmeg State looked forward to a bright future.

Did You Know?

Roger Sherman is the only American who signed all four of the important early documents of the United States: the Continental Association, the Articles of Confederation, the Declaration of Independence, and the Constitution.

JULY 16, 1787

Roger Sherman
helps write the
Connecticut Compromise.

Timeline

1614 Adriaen Block becomes the first European to explore Connecticut.

1633 Puritans establish Windsor, the first permanent settlement in Connecticut.

1637 The Pequot War ends in defeat for the Native Americans.

1639 Hartford, Windsor, and Wethersfield adopt the Fundamental Orders, forming the Connecticut Colony.

1642 The English Civil War begins.

1651 The English Civil War ends in victory for the Puritans in Parliament.

1660 England's monarchy is restored with a new king.

1665 The New Haven Colony is absorbed into the Connecticut Colony.

1687 Sir Edmond Andros fails to take Connecticut's charter, and Connecticut remains an independent colony.

1701 The Collegiate School is founded at Saybrook. It is renamed Yale College in 1718.

1763 With the help of American colonists, the English win the French and Indian War.

1764 The *Connecticut Courant* begins publication.

1775 The Revolutionary War begins.

1776 On July 4, the Declaration of Independence is signed. The British hang Patriot Nathan Hale as a spy on September 22.

1781 On September 6 the British take over Fort Griswold, and many of its defenders are slaughtered.

1783 The Treaty of Paris ends the Revolutionary War. The British officially recognize the United States as an independent nation.

1787 The Connecticut Compromise saves the Constitutional Convention.

1788 On January 9 Connecticut becomes the fifth state.

"I only lament, that I have but one life to lose for my country."

—Believed to be Nathan Hale's last words before he was hanged in 1776

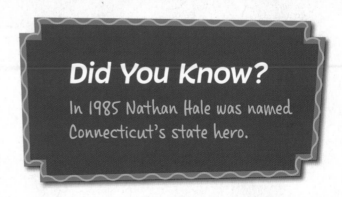

Did You Know?

In 1985 Nathan Hale was named Connecticut's state hero.

Glossary

abolish (uh-BOL-ish)—to put an end to something officially

ally (AL-eye)—a person or country that helps and supports another

ancestor (AN-sess-tuhr)—a member of a person's family who lived a long time ago

apprentice (uh-PREN-tiss)—a person who works for another to learn a trade or craft

charter (CHAR-tuhr)—an official document granting permission to set up a new colony, organization, or company

colony (KAH-luh-nee)—a place that is settled by people from another country and is controlled by that country

convert (kuhn-VURT)—to change from one religion or faith to another

gristmill (GRIST-mil)—a building for grinding grain

indentured servant (in-DEN-churd SUR-vuhnt)—a person who works for someone else for a certain period of time in return for payment of travel and living costs

indigo (IN-duh-goh)—a plant that produces a deep-blue dye

inherit (in-HER-it)—to be given someone's property after he or she dies

liberal (LIB-ur-uhl)—broad-minded and tolerant, especially of other people's ideas

Loyalist (LOI-uh-list)—a colonist who was loyal to Great Britain during the Revolutionary War

militia (muh-LISH-uh)—a group of volunteer citizens who are organized to fight but are not professional soldiers

monarchy (MON-ahr-kee)—a system of government in which the ruler is a king or queen

Patriot (PAY-tree-uht)—a person who sided with the colonies during the Revolutionary War

plantation (plan-TAY-shuhn)—a large farm where crops are raised by people who live there

Protestant (PROT-uh-stuhnt)—a Christian who does not belong to the Roman Catholic or the Orthodox Church

Puritan (PYOOR-uh-tuhn)—a follower of a strict religion common during the 1500s and 1600s; Puritans wanted simple church services and enforced a strict moral code

ratify (MON-ahr-kee)—to formally approve

smallpox (SMAWL-poks)—a disease that spreads easily from person to person, causing chills, fever, and pimples that scar

Tory (TOR-ee)—a colonist who remained loyal to the British government

traitor (TRAY-tuhr)— someone who aids the enemy of his or her country

wigwam (WIG-wahm)—a hut made of poles covered with bark, leaves, or animal skins

Critical Thinking Using the Common Core

1. How does the quote on page 16 add to your understanding of the Pequot War? (Craft and Structure)
2. Why was Connecticut called "the Land of Steady Habits?" Use evidence from the text to support your answer. (Key Ideas and Details)
3. How did Connecticut's involvement (or lack of involvement) in the Revolutionary War allow it to become a major supplier of food and supplies to the Continental army? (Integration of Knowledge and Ideas)

Read More

Alexander, Richard. *The Colony of Connecticut*. Spotlight on the 13 Colonies. New York: PowerKids Press, 2015.

Cunningham, Kevin. *The Connecticut Colony*. True Books: American History. New York: Scholastic, 2011.

Labairon, Cassandra. *Connecticut*. This Land Called America. Mankato, Minn.: Creative Education, 2009.

Internet Sites

FactHound offers a safe, fun way to find Internet sites related to this book. All of the sites on FactHound have been researched by our staff.
Here's all you do:
Visit *www.facthound.com*
Type in this code: 9781515722403

Super-cool stuff! Check out projects, games and lots more at **www.capstonekids.com**

Source Notes

Page 16, callout quote: John Underhill. *Hyatt's Photographic Reprints: Newes from America*. London: Hamilton Road, Ealing, 1891, p. 40.

Page 18, callout quote: "Abstracts of Two Sermons by Rev. Thomas Hooker from the Short-Hand Notes of Mr. Henry Wolcott." *Collections of the Connecticut Historical Society*. Vol. 1. Hartford: Connecticut Historical Society, 1860, p. 20.

Page 39, callout quote: Diana Ross McCain. *It Happened in Connecticut*. Guilford, Conn.: Globe Pequot Press, 2008, p. 42.

Page 43, callout quote: Maria Hull Campbell. "Execution of Captain Hale and Major Andre: Parallel Drawn between these Two Officers." *Revolutionary Services and Civil Life of General William Hull*. New York: D. Appleton and Co., 1848, p. 50.

Regions of the 13 Colonies

Northern Colonies	Middle Colonies	Southern Colonies
Connecticut, Massachusetts, New Hampshire, Rhode Island	Delaware, New Jersey, New York, Pennsylvania	Georgia, Maryland, North Carolina, South Carolina, Virginia
land more suitable for hunting than farming; trees cut down for lumber; trapped wild animals for their meat and fur; fished in rivers, lakes, and ocean	the "Breadbasket" colonies—rich farmland, perfect for growing wheat, corn, rye, and other grains	soil better for growing tobacco, rice, and indigo; crops grown on huge farms called plantations; landowners depended heavily on servants and slaves to work in the fields

Select Bibliography

"Abstracts of Two Sermons by Rev. Thomas Hooker from the Short-Hand Notes of Mr. Henry Wolcott." *Collections of the Connecticut Historical Society*. Vol. 1. Hartford: Connecticut Historical Society, 1860.

Campbell, Maria Hull. "Execution of Captain Hale and Major Andre: Parallel Drawn between these Two Officers." *Revolutionary Services and Civil Life of General William Hull*. New York: D. Appleton and Co., 1848.

Grant, Ellsworth S. "The Main Stream of New England." *American Heritage*, April 1967, 46–58, 100–105.

McCain, Diana Ross. *It Happened in Connecticut*. Guilford, Conn.: Globe Pequot Press, 2008.

Reader's Digest. *Family Encyclopedia of American History*. Pleasantville, N.Y.: Reader's Digest Association, 1975.

Rowse, A.L. "Pilgrims and Puritans." *American Heritage*, October 1959, 48–52, 78–83.

Underhill, John. *Hyatt's Photographic Reprints: Newes from America*. London: Hamilton Road, Ealing, 1891.

Virga, Vincent and Diana Ross McCain. *Connecticut: Mapping the Nutmeg State Through History*. Guilford, Conn.: Globe Pequot Press, 2011.

Index

Andros, Edmund, 24, 42
Arnold, Benedict, 36–38
Articles of Confederation, 40

Block, Adriaen, 14, 42
Bushnell, David, 35

Canada, 4, 36
Charter Oak, 24, 25
Connecticut Courant, 31, 32, 42

daily life, 11–12
Davenport, John, 17
diseases, 13

England, 4, 5, 6, 9, 13, 19, 20, 25,
    32, 34, 42
English Civil War, 19, 42
English kings
    Charles II, 19, 20
    James II, 24
Eyre, Colonel, 36

farming, 5, 6, 8, 11, 25, 29, 30, 32, 39, 46
forts
    Griswold, 36, 37, 38, 39, 43
    Trumbull, 36
Fundamental Orders, 18, 25, 42

Germany, 6

Hale, Nathan, 35, 42, 43
Hartford, 14, 15, 20, 24, 25, 42
Hooker, Thomas, 15, 18

Ireland, 6

Ledyard, William, 38, 39

manufacturing, 8, 26
Mason, John, 16
Middle Colonies, 8, 46
Mohegans, 10, 11, 13, 16
Montgomery, Major, 36, 38

Narragansetts, 16
Netherlands, 6, 14
New England, 8, 24
New Haven, 10, 17, 19, 20, 21, 22,
    25, 30, 42

Nipmunks, 10
Northern Colonies, 8, 22, 24, 38, 46

Occom, Samson, 13

Paugussetts, 10
Pequots, 10, 13, 16, 17
Pequot War, 16, 42
Podunks, 10
Poquonnocs, 10

Quinnipiacs, 10

religions, 13, 15, 17, 31
Revolutionary War, 33, 34–39, 42–43

Saybrook, 19, 23, 30, 42
Scotland, 6
Sherman, Roger, 40
Siwanogs, 10
slavery, 25
Sons of Liberty, 33
Southern Colonies, 8, 25, 46
Stamp Act, 32, 33
Sweden, 6

trades, 26–30
Trumbull, Jonathan, 39
Tunxis, 10
Turtle, 35

Underhill, John, 16
U.S. Constitution, 40

Washington, George, 39
Watson, Hannah Bunce, 32
Wethersfield, 15, 16, 42
Windsor, 15, 22, 42
Winthrop, John, Jr., 20, 23
witches, 22, 23

Yankee Peddlers, 29
Young, Alice, 22